ADVANTAGE

Pupil's Edition

Georgia Test Preparation

CRCT and Stanford 9

Includes Test Taking Tips and
math assessment items for
- multiple choice format
- short answer
- extended response

Grade 3

Harcourt Brace & Company

Orlando • Atlanta • Austin • Boston • San Francisco • Chicago • Dallas • New York • Toronto • London
http://www.hbschool.com

Printed in the United States of America

ISBN 0-15-321595-X

2 3 4 5 6 7 8 9 10 073 2002 2001

CONTENTS

Name _____

Choose the letter of the correct answer.

1
4
+5

A 6 **C** 8 **E** NOT HERE
B 7 **D** 10

Test Taking Tips

Eliminate choices.

If you solve the problem and don't see your solution listed, mark NOT HERE as the answer.

---

2 $6 - 1 = \underline{\ ?\ }$

F 0 **H** 5 **K** NOT HERE
G 3 **J** 7

3
8
−3

A 2 **C** 4 **E** NOT HERE
B 3 **D** 5

4 $7 + 2 + 5 = \underline{\ ?\ }$

F 13 **H** 15 **K** NOT HERE
G 14 **J** 16

5
47
+38

A 65 **C** 85 **E** NOT HERE
B 75 **D** 95

6
60
−37

F 43 **H** 23 **K** NOT HERE
G 33 **J** 13

7
81
−36

A 15 **C** 35 **E** NOT HERE
B 25 **D** 45

8
564
+158

F 722 **H** 622 **K** NOT HERE
G 712 **J** 613

9
$4.18
1.26
+ 6.63

A $12.07 **C** $12.97 **E** NOT HERE
B $12.27 **D** $13.06

10 Use order in addition to find the missing fact.

$$8 + 5 = 13,$$
so $\underline{\ ?\ } + \underline{\ ?\ } = \underline{\ ?\ }$

F $5 + 8 = 13$ **J** $8 + 5 = 85$
G $5 + 13 = 18$ **K** NOT HERE
H $5 + 8 = 58$

GO ON

11 Which subtraction fact is related to this addition fact?

$$7 + 6 = 13$$

A $13 - 6 = 7$
B $7 - 6 = 1$
C $13 + 6 = 19$
D $13 + 7 = 20$

12 Estimate the sum by rounding.

$$\begin{array}{r} 22 \\ +51 \\ \hline \end{array}$$

F 70   **H** 90
G 80   **J** 100

13 Linda has 14 red bows and 27 yellow bows for her hair. How many bows does she have in all? Is this number even or odd?

A 31 bows; even
B 31 bows; odd
C 41 bows; even
D 41 bows; odd

14 One day, 17 students were eating lunch. Then 4 students went out to play. How many students were still eating lunch?

F 3 students
G 12 students
H 13 students
J 15 students

15 Kim has 40 animals on her farm. Of these, 17 are cows. The rest are sheep. How many sheep are on Kim's farm?

A 3 sheep   **C** 17 sheep
B 13 sheep   **D** 23 sheep

16 James had some money. His father gave him $2.00 more. James bought a game for $4.00 and a toy car for $2.50. He now has $1.50 left. How much money did James have to begin with?

F $1.00
G $5.00
H $6.00
J $8.25

17 Kim's grandparents live 400 miles away. Her aunt and uncle live 263 miles closer. How many miles away do her aunt and uncle live?

A 37 miles
B 137 miles
C 139 miles
D 317 miles

18 During one month, 185 tickets were sold at Game A, 234 tickets were sold at Game B, and 168 tickets were sold at Game C. How many tickets were sold at all three games?

F 577 tickets
G 587 tickets
H 684 tickets
J 5,187 tickets

19 $$\begin{array}{r} 821 \\ -379 \\ \hline \end{array}$$

A 334   **C** 442
B 432   **D** 552

Name _____

20 Jaime started out with 16 white socks. Later, he had only 9 white socks. How many socks got lost?

On the lines below, explain how you figured out the answer.

_____

_____

_____

_____

Test Taking Tips

What do you know about fact families that will help you solve the problem?

---

21 Tara has 15 crayons. Her friend Ellen has none. Tara wants to share as equally as possible, but she does not want to break any of the crayons.

Find two ways that Tara can share her crayons with Ellen. Write number sentences to show how you solved the problem.

Test Taking Tips

What do you know about fact families that will help you solve this problem?

_____

_____

GO ON ▶

Name _____

22 Marie has 4 boxes of holiday decorations. The first box holds 18 items. The second one holds 22 items. The third box holds 9 items. The fourth one holds 12 items.

About how many holiday decorations does Marie have? Explain the strategy you used to make your estimate.

_____

_____

_____

_____

_____

_____

 **Test Taking Tips**

How can rounding up and rounding down help you solve the problem?

23 Ms. Sampson gave out 105 pencils from this box.

700
PENCILS

About how many pencils are left in the box?

_____

Explain how you found your answer.

_____

_____

_____

Test Taking Tips

Are you looking for an exact answer or an estimate?

 GO ON

Name _____

24 Keith's class of 29 students was putting on a play. There were acting roles for only 7 students. How many students will not have acting roles?

On the lines below, show your work and explain your thinking.

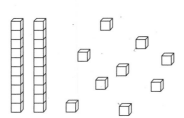

_____

_____

Think · Solve · Explain
Short Answer
Test Taking Tips

How can you use base-ten blocks to model the problem?

---

25 How much faster can the zebra run than the rabbit?

Animal	Top speed in kilometers per hour
Cheetah	112
Lion	80
Elk	72
Zebra	64
Rabbit	56
Reindeer	51

Show how you solved the problem.

_____

_____

_____

Think · Solve · Explain
Short Answer
Test Taking Tips

What information do you need from the chart before you can solve this problem?

GO ON

26 On Monday and Tuesday, the vet treated 53 dogs in all. On Monday, she treated 29 dogs. How many dogs did she treat on Tuesday?

On the lines below, explain the method you used to figure out the problem.

_____

_____

_____

_____

 Test Taking Tips

How can you restate the problem?

27 Lisa left the library and walked to the park. From there, she walked to the post office. How far did she walk?

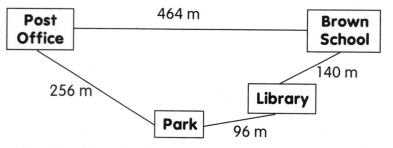

On the lines below, show your work and explain your thinking.

_____

_____

_____

Test Taking Tips

What information from the map is useful in solving this problem?

Name _____

28 **a.** Paul needs 20 pies for a party. He has baked 8 of them. His two aunts have baked 2 pies each. His mother has baked 4. Paul hopes his father will bake the rest. How many pies will his father have to bake?

Test Taking Tips

How many pies have already been baked?

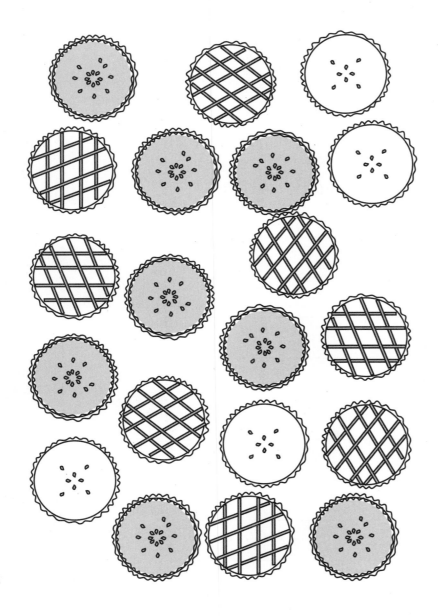

GO ON

Name _____

28 b. Write your answer on this page. Draw a picture or a diagram showing the number of pies needed and the number already baked.

Test Taking Tips

How can drawing a picture help you solve the problem?

Explain how you know your answer is right.

_____

_____

_____

_____

_____

_____

_____

GO ON

Name _____

29 a. Pablo's father wanted to treat his children to a tour of St. Augustine, Florida. He read the following sign at the tourist center:

Tours of St. Augustine, Florida

Train Tickets
Adult $7.00   Child $2.00

Horse and Carriage Rides
Adult $7.00   Child $3.00

Pablo's father paid $20 for horse and carriage tickets.

How many adults and how many children went on the ride?

Test Taking Tips

What information from the chart do you need?

© Harcourt

GO ON

Name _____

29 b. Write your answer on this page. Explain your reasoning.

_____

_____

_____

_____

_____

_____

_____

_____

_____

_____

_____

_____

_____

_____

_____

_____

_____

_____

_____

Test Taking Tips

How can you check your answer?

Math Advantage Georgia Test Prep   10

Name _____

Choose the letter of the correct answer.

For questions 1–2, tell what time it is.

1

A 6 minutes after two
B 6 minutes after three
C 23 minutes after six
D NOT HERE

Test Taking Tips

Get the information you need.
Which part tells the hour on a digital clock?

2

F 7:20   H 8:24
G 7:25   J 8:30

3 Tell how many minute marks the minute hand has moved from 12. Count by fives.

A 7 minutes
B 30 minutes
C 35 minutes
D 40 minutes

4 The hour hand on Bob's watch is a little past five. The minute hand is pointing to the 2. What time is it?

F 5:10   H 6:02
G 5:20   J 6:10

5 Tim is meeting Richard at the park at 4:15. Where will the minute hand on the clock be then?

A on the 11   C on the 6
B on the 9   D on the 3

6 Jenny's mother asked her to help cook dinner. How much time will it take Jenny to help cook dinner?

F about 3 minutes
G about 30 minutes
H about 30 hours
J about 300 hours

For questions 7–8, use the schedule.

SCHOOL FUN WEEK		
Activity	**Day**	**Time**
3-Legged Race	Monday	9:00–9:30
Tug-of-War	Tuesday	10:00–10:30
100-m Race	Wednesday	8:30–?
Balloon Toss	Thursday	11:00–11:30
200-m Race	Friday	11:30–12:00

7 The 100-meter race lasts for 1 hour and 30 minutes. At what time does it end?

A 8:30   C 10:00
B 9:00   D 10:30

GO ON

8 Ice cream is half price at the same time that the Tug-of-War takes place. When is ice cream half price?

F Monday   9:00 – 9:30
G Tuesday   10:00 – 10:30
H Thursday   11:00 – 11:30
J Friday   11:30 – 12:00

9 When the digital clock says 8:00, what time is it?

A eight o'clock
B 5 minutes after eight
C nine o'clock
D NOT HERE

10 Count the money.

F $1.21   H $1.31
G $1.26   J $1.36

11 $32.67
      + 14.82

A $46.39   C $47.39
B $46.49   D $47.49

12 $7.65
      − 0.82

F $5.82   H $6.83
G $6.73   J NOT HERE

13 Pam spends $6.25 for a theme park ticket, $1.50 for chips, and $2.50 for a puzzle. How much money does she spend in all?

A $10.25   C $9.00
B $9.25   D NOT HERE

For questions 14–15, use the calendar.

June

Sun	Mon	Tue	Wed	Thu	Fri	Sat
			1	2	3	4
5	6	7	8	9	10	11
12	13	14	15	16	17	18
19	20	21	22	23	24	25
26	27	28	29	30		

14 What is the date three weeks before June 23?

F June 1   H June 3
G June 2   J June 30

15 Sarah kept a record of the rainfall for each day starting on June 12. She kept a record for the next 11 days. What was the last day she recorded the rainfall?

A June 23   C June 28
B June 26   D June 30

© Harcourt

16 Sean's schedule for his guitar lessons was chewed up by the dog.

Guitar Lessons	
Monday	12:30
Tuesday	12:45
Wednesday	
	1:15
	1:30
Saturday	

Look for the pattern. Fill in the missing days and times.

On the lines below, explain the pattern.

_____

_____

Test Taking Tips

How can counting by 15's help you find a pattern?

---

17 On Monday, Gillian saw the sunrise at 6:30 A.M. That evening, she saw the sunset at 6:48 P.M.

How many hours and minutes of daylight were there on Monday?

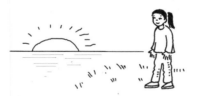

_____

On the lines below, explain how you solved the problem.

_____

_____

_____

Test Taking Tips

What are you trying to find out? Restate the problem in your own words.

GO ON

18 Cheryl has been waiting to use a treadmill, but all the treadmills are in use. It is now 4:17.

This chart is posted near the treadmills. How much longer will Cheryl have to wait before she can begin her exercise?

Treadmill Sign-up Sheet
Time Limit: 30 minutes

Name	Start Time
Dwaine	4:08
Suzanne	3:50
Oscar	4:15
Loretta	3:59

Explain how you figured out the answer.

_____

_____

Test Taking Tips

How can finding each stop time help you solve the problem?

19 Elizabeth bought a baseball bat for $17.23. She gave the cashier $20.00. How much change should Elizabeth get back? What coins and bills could the cashier use to give this change to Elizabeth?

On the lines below, explain how you solved the problem.

_____

_____

Test Taking Tips

How can acting it out help you solve this problem?

GO ON

20 The chart shows the ways Carla can earn money.

Carla wants to buy a ticket to go to the circus. Tickets cost $8.75. How many times will she have to wash the dishes to earn enough for a circus ticket?

Ways to Earn Money	
Sweep kitchen floor	$1.00
Mow lawn	$2.35
Wash dishes	$1.50
Walk the dog	$2.00

On the lines below, explain how you solved the problem.

_____

_____

Test Taking Tips

What operation can you use to solve the problem?

---

21 Marco was looking for some camping gear. One store advertised the following prices:

Camping Gear	
Backpack	$9.67
Flashlight	$8.85
Food Cooler	$6.69
Air Mattress	$7.98

Which item is least expensive?

Which item is most expensive?

On the lines below, explain how you know.

_____

_____

Test Taking Tips

How can ordering prices from most to least help you solve this problem?

GO ON

Name _____

22 Julio chose a sweater for $19.95, pants for $14.96, and 2 pairs of socks for $4.95 each. ESTIMATE how much money he will need to pay for them.

$19.95

$14.96

 $4.95

$4.95

Test Taking Tips

How can rounding to the nearest dollar help you solve the problem?

On the lines below, explain the steps you followed to find the answer.

_____

_____

_____

23 Anthony went to the bookstore and picked out these three books.

$11.88 $4.06 $3.30

Test Taking Tips

What are you trying to find out? Restate the problem in your own words.

Anthony has $20. Does he have enough money to buy the three books?

Use words and numbers to explain your thinking.

_____

_____

_____

GO ON

24 **a.** Kristin looked at the clock at 5:30. She realized that her birthday party would be over in 30 minutes. It started three hours ago.

Test Taking Tips

How can drawing a picture help you solve the problem?

Draw hands on the clock faces. On one, show the time the party started. On another, show the time Kristin looked at the clock. On the third, show the time the party will be over.

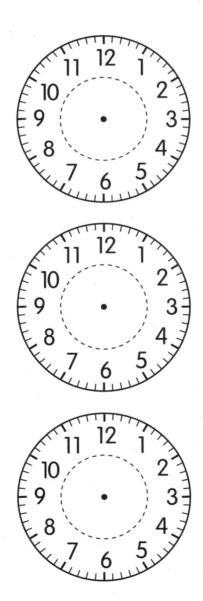

GO ON

Name _____

24 **b.** At what time did the party start? _____ : _____

At what time did Kristin look at the clock? _____ : _____

At what time did the party end? _____ : _____

Explain how you checked your answer.

_____

_____

_____

_____

_____

_____

_____

_____

_____

_____

_____

_____

_____

_____

Test Taking Tips

How can rereading the question help you check your answer?

© Harcourt

GO ON ➡

Name _____

25 a. Brian made tally marks on a chart as he counted the change in his pockets.

Half Dollars	Quarters	Dimes	Nickels	Pennies
|||	~~||||~~	~~||||~~ ||	~~||||~~ ~~||||~~		|||

Does Brian have enough money to buy a baseball cap for $4.95? If so, how much will he have left over? If not, how much more money does he need?

25 b. Write your answers on this page. Show your work and explain your reasoning.

Be sure that your explanation is clear and complete.

_____

_____

_____

_____

_____

_____

_____

_____

_____

_____

_____

_____

_____

_____

_____

_____

_____

STOP

Name _____

Choose the letter of the correct answer.

1 How many  are there in ?

A 10　　　　C 70
B 50　　　　D 100

Test Taking Tips

Understand the problem.
How could you use skip-counting to find the answer?

---

2 How many nickels are equal to one dime?

F 1　　　　H 10
G 2　　　　J 25

For questions 3–4, use the calendar.

April

Sun	Mon	Tue	Wed	Thu	Fri	Sat
		1	2	3	4	5
6	7	8	9	10	11	12
13	14	15	16	17	18	19
20	21	22	23	24	25	26
27	28	29	30			

3 What is the date of the fifth Tuesday?

A April 8　　　C April 23
B April 15　　　D April 29

4 How many Fridays are in the month?

F 2 Fridays　　　H 4 Fridays
G 3 Fridays　　　J 5 Fridays

5 What is the value of the 5 digit in 562?

A 5　　　　C 500
B 50　　　　D 5,000

For questions 6–7, use patterns of tens to find the sum or difference.

6 37 + 30 = ___?___

F 40　　　　H 57
G 47　　　　J 67

7 95 − 40 = ___?___

A 25　　　　C 40
B 35　　　　D 55

8 Jess is holding 5 coins in her hand. The coins are worth 47 cents. Which set of coins is Jess holding?

F 2 quarters, 2 nickels, 1 penny
G 1 quarter, 2 dimes, 2 pennies
H 1 quarter, 2 dimes, 1 penny
J NOT HERE

For questions 9–10, use patterns of hundreds or thousands to find the sum or difference.

9 734 − 400

A 334　　　　C 534
B 434　　　　D 637

GO ON

10 4,503 + 2,000

F 2,503   H 6,503
G 4,505   J 7,503

11 What number is six thousand nine hundred forty-six?

A 6,694   C 9,264
B 6,946   D 9,462

12 What is the number?

50,000 + 8,000 + 100 + 20 + 7

F 51,127   H 58,712
G 58,127   J NOT HERE

For questions 13–14, use the table.

Classes in Oak Hill School are collecting soup labels to buy a jungle gym for their school.

SOUP LABEL COLLECTION	
Room Number	Number of Soup Labels
12	8,000
13	12,000
14	16,000
15	6,500
16	18,000

13 Room helpers have picked up labels in rooms that have collected more than 15,000 labels. Which two rooms have the room helpers picked up labels from?

A Rooms 13 and 14
B Rooms 13 and 16
C Rooms 14 and 16
D Rooms 15 and 16

14 It will take about 1 hour to count 1,000 labels. About how long will it take to count the labels in Room 13?

F about 1 hour
G about 12 hours
H about 120 hours
J about 1,200 hours

15 Which answer shows the numbers in order from least to greatest?

528, 544, 488

A 544, 528, 488
B 528, 544, 488
C 488, 544, 528
D 488, 528, 544

16 Use the number line. Which two tens is the number 48 between?

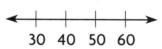

30 40 50 60

F 20–30   H 40–50
G 30–40   J NOT HERE

17 Round the number 780 to the nearest hundred.

A 500   C 700
B 600   D 800

18 Compare the numbers. Choose <, >, or =.

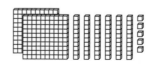

265 ● 256

F <   G =   H >

19 What is the value of each digit in 405?

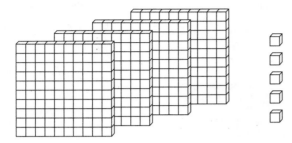

On the lines below, explain how you know.

_____

_____

_____

_____

Solve • Explain
Think

Short
Answer

**Test
Taking
Tips**

How can you use place value to answer the question?

20 Madison School took a survey to find out how students get to school. How many third graders do NOT walk to school? Show how you solved the problem. Use numbers and words.

How Third Graders Get to School	
Ride the bus	18
Walk	12
Ride bikes	14
Ride in a car	11

Solve • Explain
Think

Short
Answer

**Test
Taking
Tips**

What information in the chart can help you solve the problem?

_____

_____

_____

GO ON

21 The odometer in Mr. Langley's car read 6,592 when he bought gas. The next time he looked at the odometer, it read 6,792. How many miles had he driven since he bought gas?

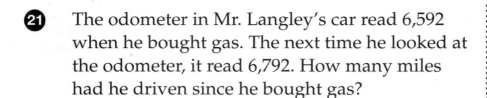

On the lines below, explain how you decided.

_____

_____

_____

Think • Solve • Explain
Short Answer

Test Taking Tips

How can using a place-value chart help you solve this problem?

---

22 Beth played soccer for 35 hours during the month of January. Lori played soccer for 53 hours. Who played more? How do you know?

On the lines below, explain how you decided.

_____

_____

_____

Think • Solve • Explain
Short Answer

Test Taking Tips

What do you know about place value that will help you solve this problem?

GO ON ➡

© Harcourt

23 The diagram shows how the first three houses on Clara's side of the block are numbered.

354   364   374   ___   ___   ___   ___

What are the house numbers for the next four houses?

On the lines below, explain how you decided on the numbers for the next four houses.

_____

_____

_____

Test Taking Tips

How can finding a pattern help you solve the problem?

---

24 Harry has to order some more horse feed, to replace what he sold in the past week. The list shows what he sold.

Horse Feed Sold

Monday	57 pounds
Tuesday	43 pounds
Wednesday	68 pounds
Thursday	32 pounds
Friday	47 pounds

On the lines below, tell if an estimate of 250 pounds is reasonable. Explain your reasoning.

_____

_____

_____

Test Taking Tips

When do you round up? When do you round down?

 25 Marvin's Food Mart is 157 miles from the town of Swanee, 261 miles from Burnic, and 176 miles from Sterling.

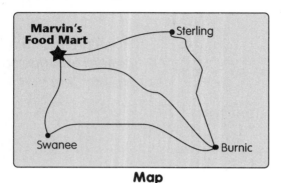

Map

Which town is closest to Marvin's Food Mart? Which one is farthest from the Mart?

On the lines below, explain how you solved the problem.

_____

_____

_____

Test Taking Tips

How can making a list help you solve the problem?

 26 The person in charge of the cafeteria kept track of the lunches sold in one day. She made this list:

Monday	700
Tuesday	767
Wednesday	576
Thursday	764
Friday	746

What was the largest number of lunches sold in one day? Explain.

_____

_____

Test Taking Tips

How can ordering the numbers help you solve the problem?

GO ON

27 **a.** Carmella started making a table to show prizes for the fair. She had to stop before she was finished.

Look for a pattern.

Help Carmella finish the table.

Number of Tickets Won	Prize Value
8	$2.00
10	$2.50
12	$3.00
14	
	$4.00
18	
20	
	$5.50

Test Taking Tips

How can finding a number pattern in each column help you complete the table?

GO ON

27 **b.** Explain how you decided to complete your table.

_____

_____

_____

_____

_____

_____

_____

_____

_____

_____

_____

_____

_____

_____

_____

_____

_____

_____

Think • Solve • Explain
Long Answer
Test Taking Tips

How can you check that your solution makes sense?

GO ON

Name _____

28 a. Koko is a gorilla who was taught sign language. The chart shows the number of signs Koko knew at various ages. One number is smudged and cannot be read.

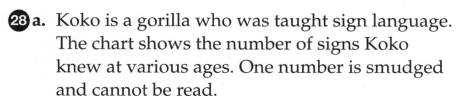

Test Taking Tips

Age in Months	Number of Signs
42	111
44	135
46	~~157~~
48	182
50	199

About how many signs does Koko learn every 2 months?

Look for a pattern in the chart.

What is a reasonable number of signs that Koko might know at 46 months?

_____

_____

_____

_____

_____

_____

_____

_____

_____

GO ON

Name _____

28 b. Explain how you decided on your answer.

Test Taking Tips

_____

_____

How can you check your work?

_____

_____

_____

_____

_____

_____

_____

_____

_____

_____

_____

_____

_____

_____

_____

Math Advantage Georgia Test Prep   30

STOP

Name _____

Choose the letter of the correct answer.

1 $1 \times 8 = \underline{\ ?\ }$

A 0   **C** 8   **E** NOT HERE
B 1   **D** 18

Test Taking Tips

Decide on a plan.
Use what you know about multiplying by 1 to solve the problem.

2
   9
$\times3$

F 12   **H** 24   **K** NOT HERE
G 18   **J** 27

3 Todd sleeps for 8 hours every night. How many hours will he sleep in 4 nights?

A 12   **C** 28   **E** NOT HERE
B 24   **D** 32

4 A cabinet had 5 shelves with 6 glasses on each shelf. How many glasses were there in all?

F 11 glasses
G 20 glasses
H 30 glasses
J 40 glasses
K NOT HERE

5 $6 \times 3 = \underline{\ ?\ }$

A 24   **C** 16   **E** NOT HERE
B 18   **D** 12

6
   7
$\times8$

F 24   **H** 40   **K** NOT HERE
G 32   **J** 56

7 $36 \div 9 = \underline{\ ?\ }$

A 3   **C** 5   **E** NOT HERE
B 4   **D** 6

8 $28 \div 7 = \underline{\ ?\ }$

F 4   **H** 6   **K** NOT HERE
G 5   **J** 7

9 $45 \div 5 = \underline{\ ?\ }$

A 6   **C** 8   **E** NOT HERE
B 7   **D** 9

10 $21 \div 7 = \underline{\ ?\ }$

F 0   **H** 2   **K** NOT HERE
G 1   **J** 3

11 Bob put cookies on a tray for a picnic. He made 3 rows with 8 cookies in each row. How many cookies were there in all?

A 24
B 36
C 48
D 54
E NOT HERE

© Harcourt

12 Which two smaller arrays can be used to find the product 6 × 7?

7
3 ☐☐☐☐☐☐☐
☐☐☐☐☐☐☐
☐☐☐☐☐☐☐

7
3 ☐☐☐☐☐☐☐
☐☐☐☐☐☐☐
☐☐☐☐☐☐☐

F 3 × 7 and 3 × 7
G 3 × 7 and 2 × 7
H 4 × 7 and 3 × 7
J 5 × 7 and 2 × 7

13 Julie put class pictures in an album. She put 9 pictures in each row. There were 3 rows. How many pictures does she have?

A 12 pictures
B 24 pictures
C 27 pictures
D 36 pictures

14 Choose the division sentence shown by the repeated subtraction.

16	12	8	4
− 4	− 4	−4	−4
12	8	4	0

F 16 ÷ 2 = 8 **H** 12 ÷ 4 = 3
G 16 ÷ 4 = 4 **J** 8 ÷ 4 = 2

15 For a party, Mrs. Holt pours 6 ounces of juice into each glass. She has a 36-ounce pitcher of juice and an 18-ounce pitcher of juice. How many glasses can she fill?

A 6 glasses **C** 8 glasses
B 7 glasses **D** 9 glasses

16 Choose the number sentence that solves the problem.

Students in a craft class are making clowns. They need 4 pieces of yarn for each clown. How many pieces of yarn do they need for 6 clowns?

F 6 × 4 = 24
G 6 + 4 = 10
H 6 ÷ 2 = 3
J 6 − 4 = 2

17 Use the number line.

0   3   6   9   12

6 × 2 = ?

A 21 **C** 16
B 18 **D** 12

18 What is the missing number for each number sentence?
5 × ? = 35   35 ÷ 5 = ?

F 6 **H** 8
G 7 **J** 9

19 ◯ ◯ ◯ ◯

4 ÷ 4 = ?

A 0 **C** 2
B 1 **D** 5

20 Beth has 16 small dolls. She placed an equal number of dolls in each of 4 piles. How many dolls were in each pile?

F 2 dolls **H** 6 dolls
G 4 dolls **J** 8 dolls

© Harcourt

21 Marly can write her name 4 times in 1 minute. How many times can she write it in 4 minutes?

Marly

Explain how you solved the problem.

_____

_____

_____

Test Taking Tips

How can using a multiplication table help you solve this problem?

22 Helena wanted to buy 4 muffins for each person in her family. There are 6 people in her family. How many muffins should she buy?

Use words and pictures to explain your answer.

_____

_____

_____

Test Taking Tips

How can drawing a picture help solve the problem?

What operation can you use to solve the problem?

© Harcourt

GO ON

23 The elevator in the apartment building takes 7 seconds to move from one floor to the next.

How long will it take to travel from Floor 2 to Floor 7?

Explain how you found your answer.

_____

_____

_____

Test Taking Tips

What do you need to figure out first?

24 Jamal noticed a pattern in these numbers.

6, 12, 18, 24, 30,…

What would be the next three numbers in the pattern?

_____

Describe the pattern that helps you predict the next numbers.

_____

_____

_____

_____

Test Taking Tips

How is each number related to the number that comes before it?

25 There are 4 basketball teams at Hightower School. Each team has 9 players. How many basketball players are there in all? Explain how you know your answer is correct.

_____

_____

_____

Test Taking Tips

What operation can you use to solve the problem?

26 William poured nickels into a coin-counting machine. The machine said he had 45¢.

How many nickels did William pour into the machine?

_____

Explain how you know.

_____

_____

_____

Test Taking Tips

How could counting by fives help you solve the problem?

Could you use an operation?

Name _____

27 Selena is arranging 72 cookies on a plate. Each row has 8 cookies. How many rows of cookies can she make?

Test Taking Tips

How can making an array help you solve this problem?

On the lines below, explain the method you used to figure out the problem.

_____

_____

_____

_____

28 What calculator key is missing?

  ?

How did you decide?

_____

_____

_____

Test Taking Tips

How does the answer in the display compare to the numbers on the left side of the equation?

© Harcourt

Name _____

29 a. Keesha runs a day-care center. She needs to buy equipment for four play groups. Each group needs a baseball, a soccer ball, and a kite. About how much money does she need for each play group?

Baseball	Soccer Ball	Kite
$2.15	$1.99	$2.75

Test Taking Tips

How can rounding to the nearest dollar help you find the answers?

© Harcourt

GO ON

Name _____

29 **b.** Write your answers on this page. Show your work and explain your reasoning.

How can using a multiplication table help?

_____

_____

_____

_____

_____

_____

_____

_____

_____

_____

30 a. Jolene has 12 erasers in her store. She wants to charge 5¢ for each eraser. She is deciding how many erasers she will put in each package.

Test Taking Tips

How can you use the picture to help solve the problem?

Help Jolene find three different ways to divide the 12 erasers into packages, ending up with no leftovers. Record your ideas below.

Number of Packages	Number of Erasers in One Package	Price per Package
		¢
		¢
		¢

GO ON

30 b. Explain how you made packages with no leftovers. How did you price the packages? Use pictures, words, and numbers.

How can you make a list to solve the problem?

Choose the letter of the correct answer.
For questions 1–2, use the pictograph.

OUR FAVORITE WHEEL RIDES

Bicycle	
Skates	
Wagon	
Skateboard	

Key: Each stands for 3 votes.

Test Taking Tips

Get the information you need.
Use the key to find out how many votes
each wheel stands for.

1 How many students like skates best?

A 6 students   **C** 12 students
B 9 students   **D** NOT HERE

2 How many more students like
bicycles than like wagons?

F 1 more   **H** 6 more
G 3 more   **J** 9 more

For questions 3–5, use the table.

CARS IN A CAR SHOW

Kind	Black	White	Red	Blue
Vans	0	2	1	5
Sports Cars	2	1	4	0
Luxury Cars	3	2	1	4

3 How many red sports cars were
there?

A 2   **B** 3   **C** 4   **D** NOT HERE

4 What was the most popular color
for the cars there?

F black   **H** red
G blue   **J** white

5 How many vans were white or
blue?

A 6   **B** 7   **C** 8   **D** NOT HERE

For questions 6–8, use the table.

STUDENTS' FAVORITE VACATION

Place	Votes
Beach	ЖЖ ЖЖ III
Theme Park	ЖЖ IIII
Campground	ЖЖ II
Home with Friends	ЖЖ I

6 How many students answered
the survey?

F 24 students   **H** 30 students
G 28 students   **J** 35 students

7 How many more students
liked the beach than liked
a campground?

A 2 more   **C** 6 more
B 4 more   **D** 8 more

8 What place did the most students
like?

F beach   **H** campground
G theme park   **J** home

Name _____

For questions 9–11, use the bar graph.

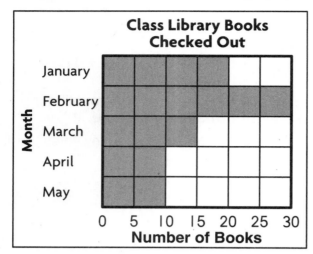

Class Library Books Checked Out

Month:
- January
- February
- March
- April
- May

Number of Books: 0 5 10 15 20 25 30

9 How many more books were checked out in February than in April?

A 5 more books
B 10 more books
C 15 more books
D 20 more books

10 In what month were the most books checked out?

F January   H March
G February   J April

11 How many more books were checked out in January than in April?

A 5 more books
B 10 more books
C 15 more books
D 20 more books

12 Which event is possible?

F Someone will read a book.
G You will grow 3 feet in a day.
H Someone will take a boat to the moon.
J The sun will not rise and set.

For questions 13–15, use the spinner.

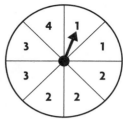

13 Which event is most likely to happen when spinning the pointer on this spinner?

A spinning a 1
B spinning a 2
C spinning a 3
D spinning a 4

14 Which event is least likely to happen when spinning the pointer on this spinner?

F spinning a 1
G spinning a 2
H spinning a 3
J spinning a 4

15 Is the spinner fair?

A yes
B no

16 Carl is playing a game. He has blue marbles, red marbles, and green marbles in a bag. Which color marble is it impossible for Carl to pull out of the bag?

F green
G blue
H red
J yellow

Math Advantage Georgia Test Prep   42   **GO ON** ➤

17 The third graders took a survey to find out what people wanted to eat at the picnic. 16 people wanted sandwiches, 24 wanted fried chicken, 9 wanted hamburgers, and 12 wanted fruit salad.

Complete the table. Use tally marks that show the information.

Third Graders' Favorite Picnic Food	
Sandwiches	
Chicken	
Hamburgers	
Fruit Salad	

On the lines, explain why the table shows the same information as in the paragraph above.

_____

_____

Test Taking Tips

How can counting by 5's help you check your work?

18 The third graders voted on their favorite pets. The chart shows the results of the vote.

Favorite Pets	Number of Students
Fish	3
Turtles	8
Cats	23
Hamsters	15
Iguanas	11
Rabbits	19
Dogs	38

Jana, a new student, was not there when the others voted. Based on the data in the chart, what do you predict will be Jana's favorite pet? Explain how you decided.

_____

_____

_____

Test Taking Tips

How can making a list help you solve the problem?

GO ON

19 The third-graders voted on the kind of chips they wanted at lunch. Here are the results:

Brand of Chips	Number of Votes	Price
Wavy	23	21 cents
Light 'n' Salty	13	36 cents
Crispy	45	27 cents
Goodies	61	23 cents
Toasties	27	18 cents
Ring-a-Ling	48	25 cents

Which three brands should the school order? Circle them.

On the lines below, explain your choice.

_____

_____

Test Taking Tips

Is there more than one right answer?

20 The third graders used tally marks to keep track of the weather for a month. This is what their tally marks looked like:

Weather in May	
Sunny days	ЖҜ ЖҜ
Rainy days	ЖҜ III
Windy days	ЖҜ IIII
Cloudy days	IIII

Make a bar graph. Explain how your bar graph shows the same information.

Weather in May

Weather											
Sunny days											
Rainy days											
Windy days											
Cloudy days											

0 1 2 3 4 5 6 7 8 9 10

Number of Days

Test Taking Tips

What does each box on the bar graph stand for?

GO ON

Name _____

21 Kareem has a bag of marbles. There are 68 blue marbles, 38 red marbles, 10 yellow marbles, and 3 black marbles. He takes out a handful of 4 marbles. Which marbles could be in his handful?

Combination	Possible	Impossible
2 blue, 1 red, 1 black		
4 yellow		
1 green, 3 black		
4 black		

_____

_____

_____

Test Taking Tips

How can making a list of the marbles help solve the problem?

22 Nathan has reading, math, and science homework. He needs to decide which assignment to do first, which to do next, and which to do last.

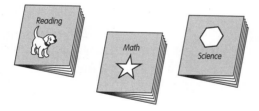

On the lines below, explain what his choices are and how you figured it out.

_____

_____

_____

_____

Test Taking Tips

How can making an organized list help you?

© Harcourt

GO ON

23 Ming-lo, Betty, Jamal, and Sara are in charge of organizing a fair. They need to form teams of two to share the work.

How many different ways can they team up?

_____

On the lines below, explain how you solved the problem.

_____

_____

_____

_____

Test Taking Tips

Think • Solve • Explain
Short Answer

How can making an organized list help you solve this problem?

24 Brent and Polly were playing a game with this spinner:

Respond to these questions.

| Red | Blue |
| Green | Yellow |

1. What are the possible outcomes of spinning on this spinner?

2. Are all possible outcomes equal? Why?

3. What are the chances of spinning green?

4. If Polly and Brent spin 40 times, what do you think their results will be?

Write your answers on the lines below.

_____

_____

_____

_____

Test Taking Tips

Think • Solve • Explain
Short Answer

How many sections are on the spinner?

Are all sections the same size?

GO ON

Name _____

25 a. Celine started this bar graph to show team scores in a sports event. Team A scored 30 points, Team B scored 50 points, and Team C scored 20 points.

Team D scored 5 points more than Team B, Team E scored 20 points more than Team C, and Team F scored 5 points less than Team A.

Figure out the scores for Team D, Team E, and Team F.

Team D Score _____

Team E Score _____

Team F Score _____

Then finish the graph.

Test Taking Tips

What information do you need to complete the graph?

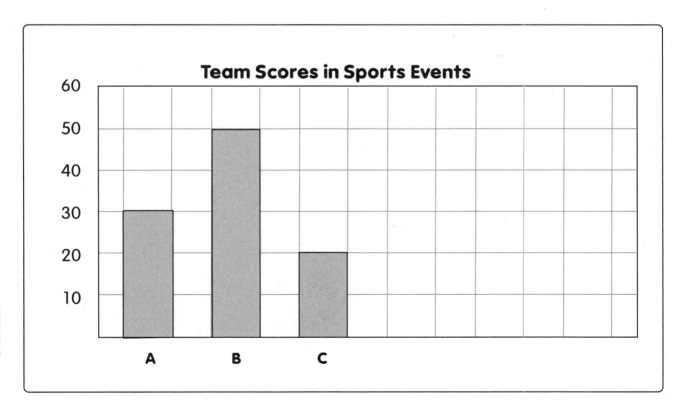

Team Scores in Sports Events

© Harcourt

GO ON

Name _____

25 b. Explain how you decided. Use numbers and words to explain your thinking.

_____

_____

_____

_____

_____

_____

_____

_____

_____

_____

_____

_____

_____

_____

Test Taking Tips

How can you check your answers?

© Harcourt

GO ON

26 a. Shaylan's class took a survey to find out how many books students read. They made this chart to show what they found out.

Books Read by Third Graders	
October	ЖГ I
November	ЖГ
December	ЖГ ЖГ I
January	ЖГ III

Make a pictograph that shows the information about books read by third graders.

In your pictograph, use this symbol to stand for 2 books:

Be sure that your pictograph has a title and a key.

Test Taking Tips

What symbol can you use to stand for less than 2 books?

26 b. Draw your pictograph here.

<table>
<tr><td colspan="2">**Books Read by Third Graders**</td></tr>
<tr><td></td><td></td></tr>
<tr><td></td><td></td></tr>
<tr><td></td><td></td></tr>
<tr><td></td><td></td></tr>
</table>

Write two sentences that compare information about books read by third graders.

_____

_____

_____

_____

_____

_____

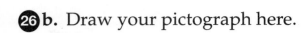

How can you check your answer?

STOP

Name _____

Choose the letter of the correct answer.

1 Is the figure formed by only straight lines, only curved lines, or both straight and curved lines?

A only straight lines
B only curved lines
C both curved and straight lines

Multiple Choice · Think · Solve · Explain

Test Taking Tips

Look for important words.
What key words could you look for to give you clues?

---

2 Identify the solid figure that is like the object shown.

F sphere
G cone
H cube
J cylinder

3 Which solid figure is like a book?

A cylinder   **C** cone
B sphere   **D** NOT HERE

4 Which solid figure has the face shown?

F cylinder
G cube
H cone
J NOT HERE

5 Which figure answers the riddle?

I am a solid figure with no edges and no faces. What am I?

A cube
B square prism
C sphere
D NOT HERE

6 Which term names the picture?

F line   **H** triangle
G line segment   **J** right angle

7 How many line segments are in a square?

A 2   **B** 3   **C** 4   **D** 5

For questions 8–9, use the grid showing the design of a kitchen. What object is located at each ordered pair?

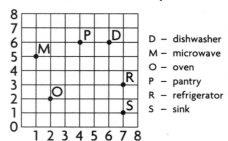

D – dishwasher
M – microwave
O – oven
P – pantry
R – refrigerator
S – sink

8 (1,5)

F oven   **H** microwave
G pantry   **J** dishwasher

9 (6,6)

A dishwasher   **C** refrigerator
B pantry   **D** sink

GO ON

For questions 10–11, decide which motion was used to move the plane figure.

10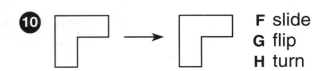

F slide
G flip
H turn

11

A slide
B flip
C turn

12 What is the next shape in the pattern?

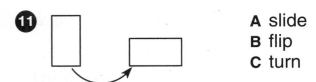

F △   G ▱   H ⬡   J □

13 Which figure is congruent to the figure shown?

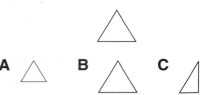

A △   B △   C ◿

14 A solid figure has 5 blocks in the first layer, 4 blocks in the second layer, and 3 blocks in the third layer. Which of these could be the solid figure?

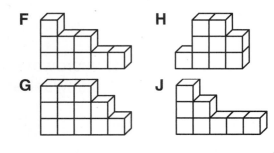

F   H
G   J

15 How many lines of symmetry does the figure have?

A 0   B 1   C 4   D 5

16 Suki drew this figure. She matched it to make the other half. How does the completed figure look?

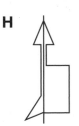

F    H

G   J

17 Which letter does not have a line of symmetry?

A A   C R
B O   D W

18 Are the solid figures congruent?

 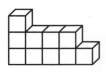

F yes   G no

© Harcourt

19 Find the name of a geometric solid in the Word Box to describe each object. Write the name on the line. Use each word once.

A. a cereal box

_____

B. a soccer ball

_____

Word Box

| cylinder cone |
| sphere rectangular prism |

C. a Native American tepee _____

D. a roll of pennies _____

In the space below, draw and label a picture of each shape.

Test Taking Tips

How can picturing the objects in your mind help you solve the problem?

20 Describe each shape. Complete the table.

Shape	Number of Sides	Number of Corners
Triangle		
Rectangle		
Square		

On the lines below, explain how two triangles or two rectangles or two squares can be different from each other.

_____

_____

_____

Test Taking Tips

How can drawing a picture help you solve this problem?

Name _____

21 Connor made a design with a triangular pattern of stars. Each row of the triangle had one less star than the one below it. There was one star in the top row. There were 4 rows in all. How many stars were in the triangle?

On the lines below, explain how you solved the problem.

_____

_____

_____

_____

Test Taking Tips

Think • Solve • Explain
Short Answer

How can drawing a picture help you solve the problem?

22 Look at the pattern. Draw the next two shapes that would continue the pattern.

○ △ △ △ ○ △ △ △

On the lines below, explain how you decided what the next two shapes should be. In your explanation, use the names of the shapes.

_____

_____

_____

_____

Test Taking Tips

Think • Solve • Explain
Short Answer

How can you find the pattern that repeats?

© Harcourt

GO ON ➡

23 Draw three squares on the dot paper below. Make two of them congruent. Then circle the two squares that are congruent.

. . . .

. . . .

. . . .

. . . .

On the lines below, explain why the two squares you circled are congruent. Then explain why the other one is not congruent.

_____

_____

_____

Test Taking Tips

What math word do you need to know? How can the dot paper help you draw figures that are the same size and shape?

24 Look at each pair of figures. Are they congruent?

Write your answers on the lines below. Explain why each pair is congruent or is not congruent.

_____

_____

_____

Test Taking Tips

What is true of congruent figures?

© Harcourt

GO ON

Name _____

25 The parking deck has a place to park motorcycles. Every space is filled. Ray's motorcycle is in the middle. There are 5 motorcycles to the right of Ray's.

How many motorcycles are there in all?

Draw a picture that shows how the motorcycles are parked. Use an X to represent each motorcycle. Label Ray's motorcycle.

Then explain the steps you followed to figure out the answer.

_____

_____

Test Taking Tips

In your picture, what do you need to show first?

What important detail do you know that will help you solve the problem?

---

26 Opal drew the first half of these figures.

Complete the figures to make them symmetrical. Then draw all the lines of symmetry that you can find in each figure.

On the lines below, explain why each of your finished figures is symmetrical.

_____

_____

Test Taking Tips

If you held a mirror up to each unfinished edge, what would you see?

GO ON

Name _____

27 **a.** Which shape could you make with each set of sticks? Write the letter:
A. rectangle B. triangle C. square

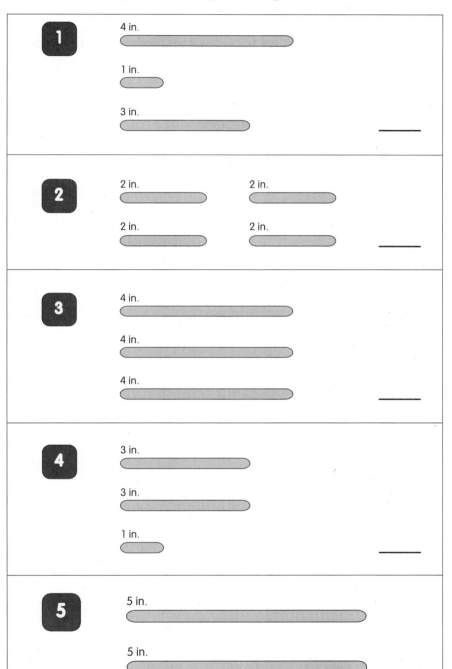

Think • Solve • Explain
Long Answer
Test Taking Tips

What do you know about rectangles, squares, and triangles?

Math Advantage Georgia Test Prep   57   **GO ON** ▶

Name _____

27 b. Draw each shape on this page. Name the shape.

Test Taking Tips

How can making a model with sticks help you solve the problem?

Explain how you know what shape could be made with each set of sticks.

_____

_____

_____

_____

GO ON

28 a. Name the shapes below and explain the differences between them.

```
┌─────────────┐        ┌──────────────────────────┐
│             │        │                          │
│      A      │        │            B             │
│             │        │                          │
└─────────────┘        └──────────────────────────┘
```

In your explanation, remember to include the number of sides, the size of the corners, and the length of the sides.

Test Taking Tips

Long Answer
Think • Solve • Explain

What is alike about the shapes? What is different about them?

GO ON

Name _____

28 b. Write your answer on this page.

_____

_____

_____

_____

_____

_____

_____

_____

_____

_____

_____

_____

_____

_____

_____

_____

_____

_____

Test Taking Tips

How can you check that your explanation is clear and complete?

Name _____

Choose the letter of the correct answer.

For questions 1–2, use the picture.

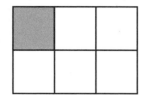

1 How many parts make up the whole?

A 4   **B** 6   **C** 8   **D** 10

Test Taking Tips

Understand the problem.
Count the total number of parts in the fraction model.

---

2 How many parts are shaded?

F 1 part   **H** 5 parts
G 2 parts   **J** 6 parts

For questions 3–4, find the numbers or words that name the part of the group that is shaded.

3

A $\frac{1}{10}$ **B** $\frac{1}{8}$ **C** $\frac{1}{6}$ **D** $\frac{1}{5}$

4

F one eighth   **H** one fourth
G one sixth   **J** one half

 5 What is the fraction in numbers?

5 out of 8

A $\frac{1}{10}$ **B** $\frac{5}{8}$ **C** $\frac{5}{6}$ **D** $\frac{3}{4}$

6 Choose <, >, or = to compare.

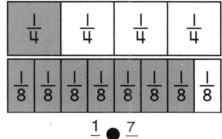

$\frac{1}{4}$ ● $\frac{7}{8}$

F <   **G** >   **H** =

7 Kelly used $\frac{4}{8}$ foot of ribbon and Danielle used $\frac{3}{4}$ foot of ribbon to wrap a gift. Who used more ribbon?

A Kelly   **B** Danielle

8 Mr. Dobins has 8 hot dogs to grill. He has grilled 4 hot dogs so far. What part of the hot dogs are grilled?

F $\frac{3}{8}$ **G** $\frac{4}{8}$ **H** $\frac{5}{8}$ **J** $\frac{6}{8}$

9 Jim poured milk in 4 of 12 cups. What part of the cups had milk?

A $\frac{2}{12}$ **B** $\frac{4}{12}$ **C** $\frac{6}{12}$ **D** $\frac{8}{12}$

GO ON

10 Which decimal names the shaded part?

F one tenth   H ten sevenths
G seven tenths J NOT HERE

11 Compare the parts of the group that are shaded. Choose <, >, or =.

$\frac{5}{8}$ ● $\frac{7}{8}$

A <   B >   C =

12 Choose <, >, or =.

$\frac{2}{3}$ ● $\frac{2}{3}$

F <   G >   H =

13 What is $\frac{6}{10}$ written as a decimal?

A 0.10   C 6.0
B 0.6   D 10.6

14 What is 0.7 written as a fraction?

F $\frac{1}{10}$ H $\frac{10}{10}$

G. $\frac{7}{10}$ J. $\frac{10}{7}$

15 What is thirty-eight hundredths written as a decimal?

A 0.38   C 38.0
B 3.80   D NOT HERE

16 What are the words for the mixed decimal 10.62?

F ten and sixty-two hundredths
G ten and six halves
H one hundred sixty-two
J NOT HERE

17 Anna ate 0.2 of her cookies and saved 0.8 of them. Did she eat more or save more?

A She ate more.
B She saved more.

18 What mixed decimal does the model show?

 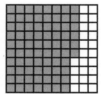

F 0.76   H 2.76
G 1.76   J 7.90

19 Wade jogged 1.8 miles on Tuesday and 1.6 miles on Thursday. On which day did he jog farther?

A Tuesday
B Thursday

GO ON

20 Five friends are covering a wall with hand-painted tiles. They have divided the wall into sections and assigned parts to each person. Here is how they divided the work:

Nate	Joe
Joe	Sasha
Joe	Sue
John	Sasha

On what fractional part of the wall is Joe working?

On the lines below, explain how you decided.

_____

_____

_____

 **Test Taking Tips**

How many parts are there in all?

21 Cassie sorted her beads in a special box. This is how she arranged them:

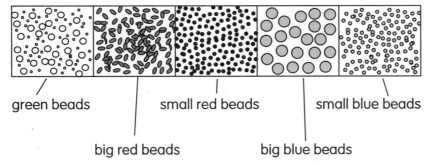

green beads   small red beads   small blue beads

big red beads   big blue beads

What fraction of the box holds blue beads? Use numbers and words. On the lines below, explain how you decided.

_____

_____

Test Taking Tips

How many equal sections does the bead case have?

How many kinds of blue beads does Cassie have?

 © Harcourt

GO ON

22 Gloria had five sections of fence to paint. By noon she had finished $3\frac{1}{3}$ of the sections.

Draw a picture to show how much Gloria has painted.

On the lines below, explain how you decided.

_____

_____

_____

Test Taking Tips

How many painted sections are completely painted? How many are partly painted?

23 Reuben is having a birthday party. He says guests will be sharing mini-pizzas. Each guest will get $1\frac{1}{4}$ pizzas.

If there are 4 people at the party, how many mini-pizzas should Reuben get?

Write your answer on the lines below. Explain how you solved the problem.

_____

_____

_____

Test Taking Tips

How can drawing a picture help you solve this problem?

GO ON

24 Quentin has finished $\frac{2}{5}$ of his math homework.

Fiona has finished $\frac{2}{3}$ of the same assignment.

Who has finished more homework?

On the lines below, explain your reasoning.

_____

_____

_____

_____

_____

_____

Test Taking Tips

How can drawing a picture for each fraction help you decide?

25 Jan paints 7 paper plates.

She paints 4 plates blue.

She paints the other plates red.

What fraction of the plates are red?

Use pictures and words to explain your thinking.

Test Taking Tips

How can drawing a picture help you see the whole group and its parts?

GO ON

26 Jake folded newspapers for his uncle. The first day, he folded 100 newspapers and was paid $5.00. The second day, he folded 150 newspapers and was paid $7.50. The third day, he folded 200 newspapers and was paid $10.00. On the fourth day, he folded 250 newspapers.

What do you think Jake was paid on the fourth day?

On the lines below, explain how you decided.

_____

_____

_____

Test Taking Tips

What is the pattern?

27 Each area of the parking lot has 10 spaces. The shaded parts of the model show how many parking spaces are taken.

Area A   **Area B**   **Area C**

Write a mixed decimal that shows how many areas of the parking lot are filled.

On the lines below, explain how you figured it out.

_____

_____

Test Taking Tips

What is a mixed decimal?

Name _____

28 a. George ate half of a pizza. Corinne ate half of a different pizza. George said that he ate more than Corinne. Corinne said they both ate the same amount because they each ate half of a pizza.

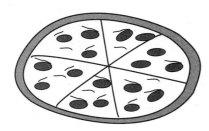

Could George be right? _____

Test Taking Tips

When is half of one thing more than half of another?

GO ON

Name _____

28 b. Use words and pictures to make your answer clear.

Be sure that your explanation is clear and complete.

_____

_____

_____

_____

_____

_____

_____

_____

_____

_____

_____

GO ON →

29 a. Ben and his mother have 12 rows of seeds to plant. Ben has completed 3 of the rows, and his mother has done 6.

Together, what fractional part of the total have they completed?

_____

GO ON

Name _____

29 b. Write your answer and explanation on this page. You might want to draw a picture to make your explanation clear.

Test Taking Tips

How can you check your answer?

Math Advantage Georgia Test Prep   70

Choose the letter of the correct answer.
You will need a ruler for some of the questions.

For questions 1–2, choose the best unit
of measure.

1 A backpack is about 15 _?_ wide.

   A inches   **C** yards
   B feet   **D** miles

Test Taking Tips

Eliminate choices.

Which units of measurement would not be
good choices?

2 Most walls are about 8 _?_ high.

   F inches   **H** yards
   G feet   **J** miles

For questions 3–4, measure the length
to the nearest half inch.

3

   A 1 in.   **C** 2 in.

   B $1\frac{1}{2}$ in.   **D** $2\frac{1}{2}$ in.

4

   F $1\frac{1}{2}$ in.   **H** $2\frac{1}{2}$ in.

   G 2 in.   **J** 3 in.

5 Brad measured the distance
from the ice cream shop to the
ski shop across the street. Which
of these was the distance
between the two shops?

   A 10 dm   **B** 10 cm   **C** 10 m

6 Which is the better estimate of a
doughnut?

   F 1 ounce   **G** 1 pound

7 What is the best estimate?

   A 18 cups   **C** 18 quarts
   B 18 pints   **D** 18 gallons

8 Which unit of measure should be
used to measure the width of a
dime?

   F centimeter
   G decimeter
   H meter

9 Which is the better estimate of
capacity?

   A 5 mL   **B** 5 L

© Harcourt

10 Which is the better unit to measure the weight of a bowling ball?

F g
G kg

For questions 11–12, use a centimeter ruler to measure the length.

11

A 1 cm   C 3 cm
B 2 cm   D 4 cm

12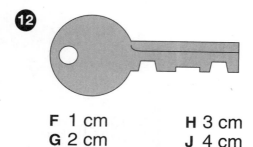

F 1 cm   H 3 cm
G 2 cm   J 4 cm

For questions 13–14, find the perimeter of the figure.

13

A 8 units   C 12 units
B 10 units   D 14 units

14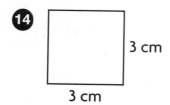

3 cm
3 cm

F 4 cm   H 10 cm
G 8 cm   J 12 cm

15 What is the perimeter of the figure?

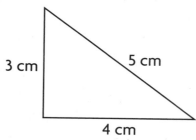

3 cm   5 cm
4 cm

A 3 cm   C 9 cm
B 6 cm   D 12 cm

16 Tom is replacing a wood frame around a window that is 7 feet high and 3 feet wide. How many feet of wood does he need?

F 10 ft   H 20 ft
G 15 ft   J 21 ft

17 What is the area of the figure in square units?

A 9 sq units   C 18 sq units
B 14 sq units   D NOT HERE

18 A rectangle has an area of 28 square feet and a side 7 feet long. What is its perimeter?

F 20 ft   H 22 ft
G 24 ft   J 26 ft

19 A rectangular pizza is 8 units long and 4 units wide. How many square units can be cut from it?

A 24 sq units   C 32 sq units
B 28 sq units   D 36 sq units

© Harcourt

GO ON

20 Patrick drove 34 miles to get to the beach. He stayed there for 3 hours and then drove home. Natalie drove 68 miles to get to the beach. She stayed there for 2 hours before driving home. How many more miles did Natalie drive than Patrick?

On the lines below, explain how you solved the problem.

_____

_____

_____

_____

Test Taking Tips

What information do you need to solve the problem?

21 Mei wants to make a poster showing five sharks. She wants to put them in order, with the longest one on top and the shortest one on bottom.

Length of Sharks	
Horn Shark	4 ft
Thresher Shark	15 ft
Great White Shark	18 ft
Basking Shark	25 ft
Mako Shark	9 ft

Number the sharks from longest to shortest.

On the lines below, explain how you know.

_____

_____

_____

Test Taking Tips

What are you trying to find out? Restate the problem in your own words.

GO ON

22 There will be eight children at Megan's party. Megan's mother will serve juice. She predicts that each child will drink about two cups of juice.

How many QUARTS of juice will she need to make?

On the lines below, show how you solved the problem. Use numbers and words.

_____

_____

_____

Test Taking Tips

How many cups are in a quart?

23 On Tuesday it was 85° at noon.

On Wednesday, the temperature was 10 degrees cooler. Show Wednesday's temperature on the blank thermometer.

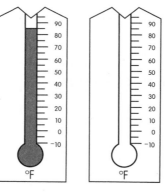

On the lines below, explain the steps you followed to figure out what the temperature was on Wednesday.

_____

_____

_____

Test Taking Tips

When it's cooler, is the temperature higher or lower?

Name _____

(24) Vinh made a bar graph showing the high temperatures for six days.

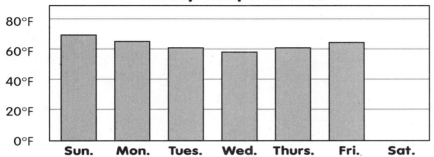

Daily Temperatures

What do you predict the temperature might be on Saturday?

On the lines below, explain how you decided.

_____

_____

Test Taking Tips

What was the highest temperature of the week? What was the lowest?

(25) Rhonda's room is 10 feet by 12 feet. She wants to put a strip of wallpaper trim around the walls near the ceiling. How many feet of wallpaper trim will she need?

On the lines below, explain how you figured out the answer.

_____

_____

_____

_____

Test Taking Tips

How can drawing a picture help you solve the problem?

Math Advantage Georgia Test Prep   75   **GO ON**

26 The picture shows the playground at Willow Park. What is the perimeter of the playground?

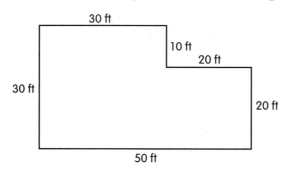

Remember, perimeter is the distance around a figure.

Write a number sentence you can use to solve the problem.

_____

Test Taking Tips

How can you use the diagram to solve the problem?

27 Randi leaves home at 3:30 P.M. and walks to the library. She spends half an hour there. Then she walks to the music store for her one-hour guitar lesson. After that, she walks home. It takes Randi 15 minutes to walk half a mile, or 30 minutes to walk a mile.

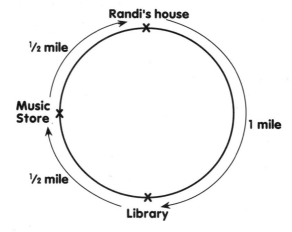

What time does Randi get home?

Explain how you know. _____

Test Taking Tips

What time does Randi get to the library? When does she leave?

Name _____

28 **a.** Marianne tried to weigh her dog, Muffin. The dog would not stay on the scale. Next she picked up Muffin and stepped on the scale, but she couldn't see the scale. Finally, she weighed herself. Then she put Muffin in the pet carrier and weighed Muffin.

The chart shows all the information she has gathered.

On the Scale	Pounds
Marianne	65
Muffin the dog	
pet carrier	5
Marianne and Muffin	
Muffin in the pet carrier	30

Use the chart. How much does Muffin weigh?

How much do Muffin and Marianne weigh together?

Test Taking Tips

What facts on the chart will help you solve the problem?

GO ON

Name _____

28 b. Explain how you solved each problem.

How much does Muffin weigh?

_____

Explain how you decided.

_____

_____

_____

_____

How much do Marianne and Muffin weigh together?

_____

Explain how you decided.

_____

_____

_____

_____

_____

Test Taking Tips

How can you check that your answers are correct?

How can you check that your explanations are clear?

GO ON ➡

Name _____

29 a. Molly has a piece of ribbon 18 cm long. She will use it to frame a picture she is drawing. The picture will be a rectangular shape.

Show two different-sized rectangular shapes that Molly could use for her drawing. Label each side with the number of centimeters.

Test Taking Tips

How can using the strategy Guess and Check help you solve the problem?

GO ON

29 b. Explain how you decided on the sizes of the rectangles. Then explain how you know both shapes are rectangles.

Long Answer

Test Taking Tips

How can you check your answer?

_____

_____

_____

_____

_____

_____

_____

_____

_____

_____

_____

_____

_____

STOP

Name _____

Choose the letter of the correct answer.

For questions 1–4, find the product. Use base-ten blocks.

1   32
   × 6

   A 182   **C** 192   **E** NOT HERE
   B 188   **D** 198

2 9 × 71 = _?_

   F 161   **H** 638   **K** NOT HERE
   G 169   **J** 639

3 9 × 14 = _?_

   A 96   **C** 136   **E** NOT HERE
   B 126   **D** 138

4   44
   × 5

   F 200   **H** 225   **E** NOT HERE
   G 220   **J** 245

5 Mrs. Lane's car goes 26 miles for each gallon of gasoline. Today she used 7 gallons. How many miles did she travel?

   A 182 miles
   B 242 miles
   C 282 miles
   D 1,413 miles
   E NOT HERE

6 47 ÷ 4 = _?_

   F 4 r7   **H** 11 r4   **K** NOT HERE
   G 11 r3   **J** 12

Test Taking Tips

Understand the problem.

How many rows of base-ten blocks would you need? How many blocks would be in each row?

7 49 ÷ 4 = _?_

   A 12 r1   **C** 13 r1   **E** NOT HERE
   B 12 r2   **D** 13 r3

8 37 ÷ 2 = _?_

   F 19 r2   **H** 18 r2   **K** NOT HERE
   G 19 r1   **J** 18 r1

9 56 ÷ 6 = _?_

   A 9   **C** 9 r2   **E** NOT HERE
   B 10 r6   **D** 9 r6

10 Mrs. Johnson had 50 balloons. She gave the same number to each of 7 children at the party. How many balloons did each child get? How many balloons were left over?

   F 7 balloons each; 0 left over
   G 7 balloons each; 1 left over
   H 8 balloons each; 1 left over
   J 8 balloons each; 3 left over
   K NOT HERE

GO ON

Name _____

For questions 11–12, choose the number sentence that correctly solves the problem.

11 In a class library, each shelf holds 15 books. There are 5 shelves. How many books are in the class library?

A $15 \div 5 = 3$ C $15 + 5 = 20$

B $15 - 5 = 10$ D $5 \times 15 = 75$

12 Each student in a class reads 4 books. There are 23 students in the class. How many books do the students read?

F $4 \times 23 = 92$
G $23 + 4 = 27$
H $23 - 4 = 19$
J $23 \div 4 = 5\ r3$

For questions 13–14, use the array. Add the two products to find the answer that completes the multiplication sentence.

13

$3 \times 16 = \underline{\ ?\ }$

A 38   C 49
B 48   D NOT HERE

14

$5 \times 13 = \underline{\ ?\ }$

F 30   H 55
G 50   J 65

15 A party table has 6 trays on it. Each tray holds 15 cookies. How many cookies are on the table?

A 60 cookies   C 95 cookies
B 90 cookies   D. 100 cookies

16 Ben's garden has 12 plants across each row. How many plants are there in 6 rows?

F 18 plants
G 62 plants
H 72 plants
J 78 plants

17 Lucy is making a quilt. The quilt will have 7 rows, with 12 squares in each row. What will the area of the quilt be?

A 84 sq units   C 94 sq units
B 89 sq units   D 104 sq units

For questions 18–19, choose whether to multiply or divide. Solve the problem.

18 A paint box has 42 tubes of paint. If 7 children share the paints, how many tubes will each child have?

F divide; 6 tubes
G divide; 9 tubes
H multiply; 294 tubes
J multiply; 296 tubes

19 Tara bought 3 skirts. Each skirt cost $19. How much did Tara spend on the skirts?

A divide; $6   C multiply; $42
B divide; $7   D multiply; $57

© Harcourt

Math Advantage Georgia Test Prep   82   GO ON

20 By Monday, the third-grade class had sold 43 magazine subscriptions. On Thursday, three students each brought in 10 more subscriptions.

How many subscriptions did the third graders sell in all?

On the lines below, explain how you solved the problem.

_____

_____

_____

_____

Test Taking Tips

How many of each base-ten block can you use to model the problem?

21 Larry earned $8.00 for mowing the neighbor's lawn. He spent $4.95 on a collection of baseball cards. Does he have enough left over to buy 5 video game tokens at 50 cents each?

$4.95 for collection

On the lines below, explain the steps you followed to solve this problem.

_____

_____

_____

_____

Test Taking Tips

What do you need to figure out first?

GO ON

Name _____

22 Read the riddle in the box.

> My perimeter is 60 inches.
> My sides are all equal.
> Draw my shape.
> How long is each side?

Illustrate and explain the answer to the riddle.

_____

_____

_____

_____

_____

Test Taking Tips

Can there be more than one answer?

---

23 Dina measured her book shelves. Each shelf is 3 feet long. There are 6 shelves in the bookcase.

Hector measured his book shelves. Each of his shelves is 24 inches long. There are 9 shelves in his bookcase.

Hector said that he had more space for books than Dina.

Is Hector right?

Remember 1 foot = 12 inches.

_____

_____

_____

Test Taking Tips

What do you need to find out first?

Name _____

24 The pictograph shows the number of bulbs Stella planted in her garden.

Bulbs in Garden	
tulips	🌷🌷🌷🌷🌷
daffodils	🌷🌷🌷
crocuses	🌷🌷🌷🌷🌷🌷🌷

Key: Each 🌷 = 12 bulbs

How many more crocuses did Stella plant than daffodils?

On the lines below, explain how you solved the problem.

_____

_____

Test Taking Tips

What do you need to find first?

25 An adult manatee weighs about 1,500 pounds. About how much would two adult manatees weigh?

Explain how you got your answer.

_____

_____

_____

Test Taking Tips

How can using mental math help you solve the problem?

GO ON

26 Calvin picked up about 19 pieces of litter in 15 minutes. Estimate how many pieces he would pick up in one hour. _____

Explain how you solved the problem.

_____

_____

_____

Test Taking Tips

How many 15-minute periods are there in one hour? How can rounding help you solve the problem?

27 For every 5 cups of juice that Julia buys, she gets a ticket for a free pretzel. Julia has collected 14 tickets.

Test Taking Tips

What operation can you use to find the answer?

How many cups of juice has Julia bought?

_____

Explain how you found your answer.

_____

_____

_____

GO ON

© Harcourt

Name _____

28 **a.** Maggie bought 3 packs of cards. Each pack had 10 cards and 3 pieces of bubble gum.

If Maggie gave 5 cards to her brother, how many cards did she have left?

Test Taking Tips

What information do you need to solve the problem?

Math Advantage Georgia Test Prep   87

GO ON

Name _____

28 b. Write your answer on this page and explain your reasoning.

_____

_____

_____

_____

_____

_____

_____

_____

_____

_____

_____

_____

_____

_____

Test Taking Tips

How can making a model help you solve the problem?

GO ON ➡

29 **a.** There are 8 jars on the art room table. Half of them are holding 10 brushes each. The rest are holding 12 brushes each.

How many more brushes are needed if 100 students want to paint?

Test Taking Tips

What do you need to figure out first?

GO ON

Name _____

29 b. Write your answer on this page. Use words and pictures to make your answer clear.

Be sure that your explanation is clear and complete.

_____

_____

_____

_____

_____

_____

_____

_____

_____

_____

_____

_____

STOP